HAWAII'S FAVORITE FISH

A coloring book that teaches you about Hawaii's fish!

Written & Illustrated
by
Sierra Maika`i Mahin

This book was colored by

This publication is a copyrighted product of © 1995 Hawaiian Service, Inc.
94-535 Uke`e Street, Waipahu, Hawaii 96797-4214
Any reproduction of all or part of this publication is prohibited without written permission of the Publisher.
10 9 8 7 6 5 4 3 2 1
Printed in Australia

A is for `Ahi.

Yellowfin Tuna   `Ahi   Thunnus albacares

`Ahi are a type of tuna fish. They can get so big that they can weigh over 300 pounds. These fast swimmers are one of Hawaii's favorite game fish. People in Hawai`i love to eat `Ahi raw as sashimi.

B is for Barracuda.

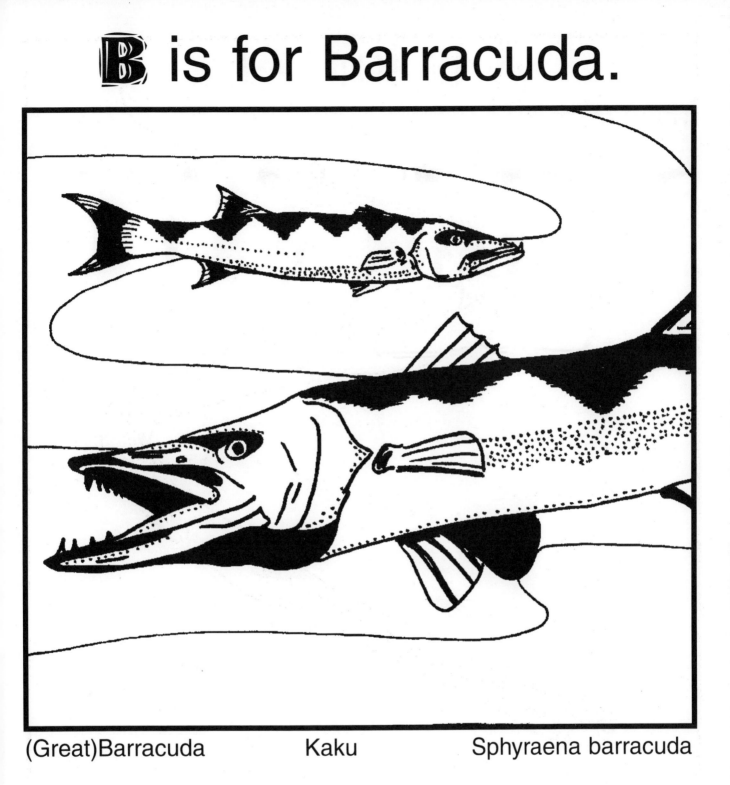

(Great)Barracuda   Kaku   Sphyraena barracuda

Barracuda are called Kaku in Hawai`i. Their powerful bodies and razor-sharp teeth make them ideal predators. Kaku can grow up to 6 feet in length. Young Kaku stay close to shore, but as they get older, they move into deeper waters.

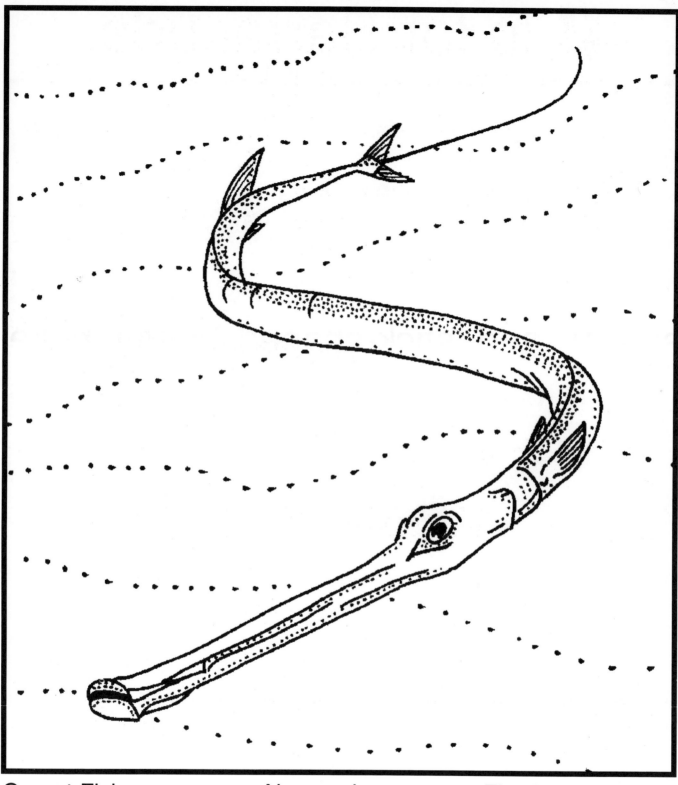

Cornet Fish   Nunu peke   Fistularia petimba

C is for Cornet Fish.

C is for Cornet Fish.

Nunu peke is the Hawaiian name for Cornet Fish. Their bodies are long, skinny, and stick-shaped. Nunu peke have a tube-like snout with a tiny mouth at the end. These unusual mouths are used to suck up small fish.

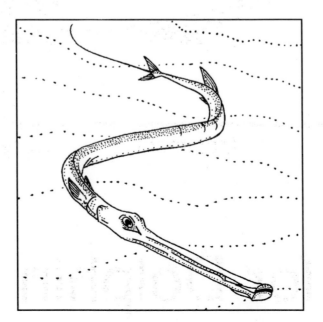

Dolphin Fish   Mahimahi   Coryphaena hippurus

D is for Dolphin Fish.

D is for Dolphin Fish.

In Hawai`i, Dolphin Fish are called Mahimahi. While they are both beauti- fully colored, the males have square heads and the females have round heads. Mahimahi can swim at 40 miles an hour and can even catch flying fish.

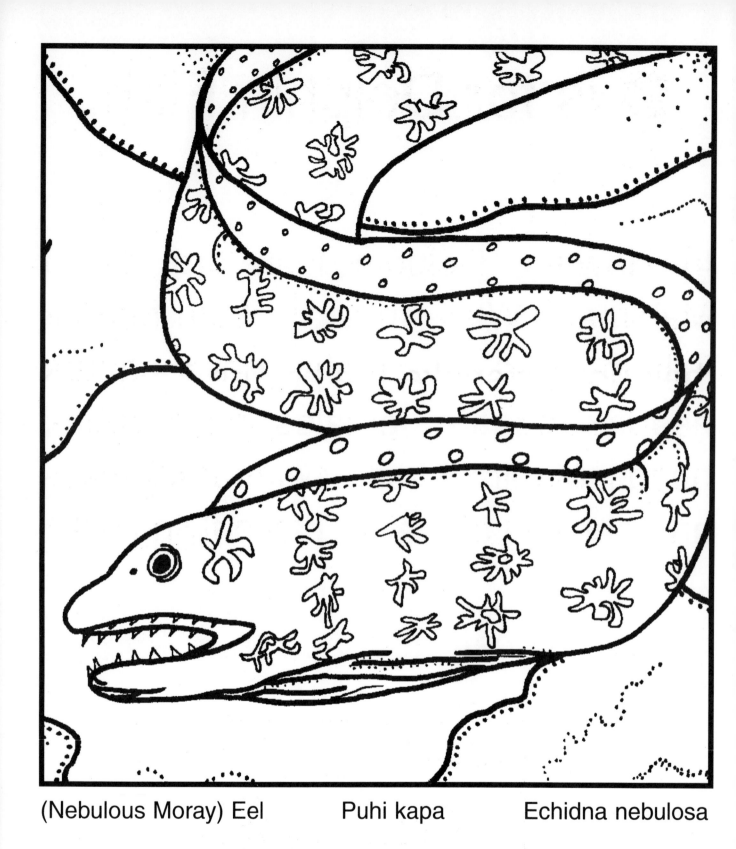

(Nebulous Moray) Eel   Puhi kapa   Echidna nebulosa

E is for Eel.

E is for Eel.

Eels, or Puhi as they are called in Hawai`i, do not look like fish because of their unique snake-like bodies. They are known for their strong jaws and teeth and often live in holes in coral or rocks. This is why when you are at the beach, you should never stick your hands where you can not see. Your fingers might be bitten.

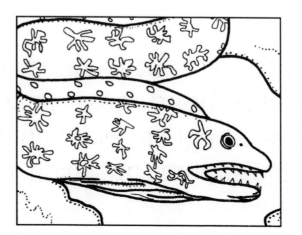

F is for Flounder.

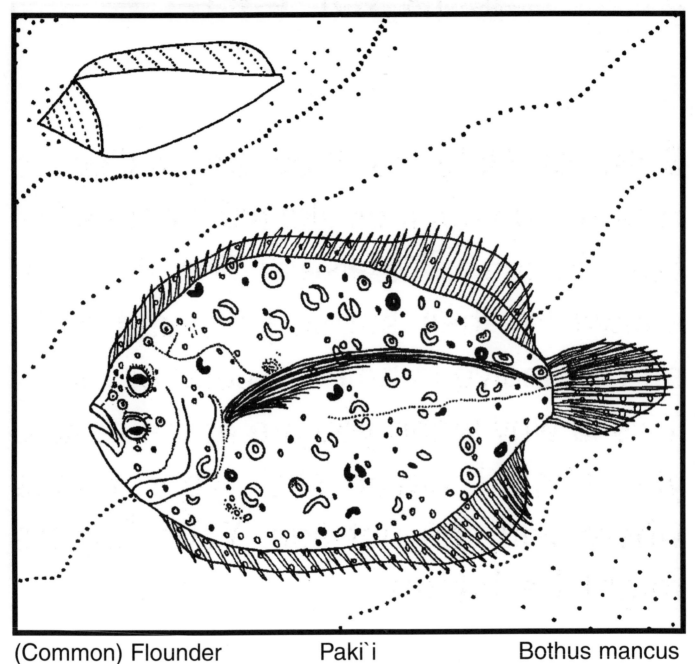

(Common) Flounder   Paki`i   Bothus mancus

When Paki`i become adults one eye moves to the other side of the head next to the other eye. Paki`i then turn and begin to swim on their sides. They can lie flat on the bottom and hide in the sand and seaweed.

G is for Grouper.

(Seale's) Grouper   Hapu`upu`u   Epinephelus quernus

These grouchy looking Sea Bass, or Hapu`upu`u, have enormous mouths and can swallow fish in one gulp. They are purplish brown and covered with white spots. Hapu`upu`u are very large fish. The largest on record weighed 563 pounds.

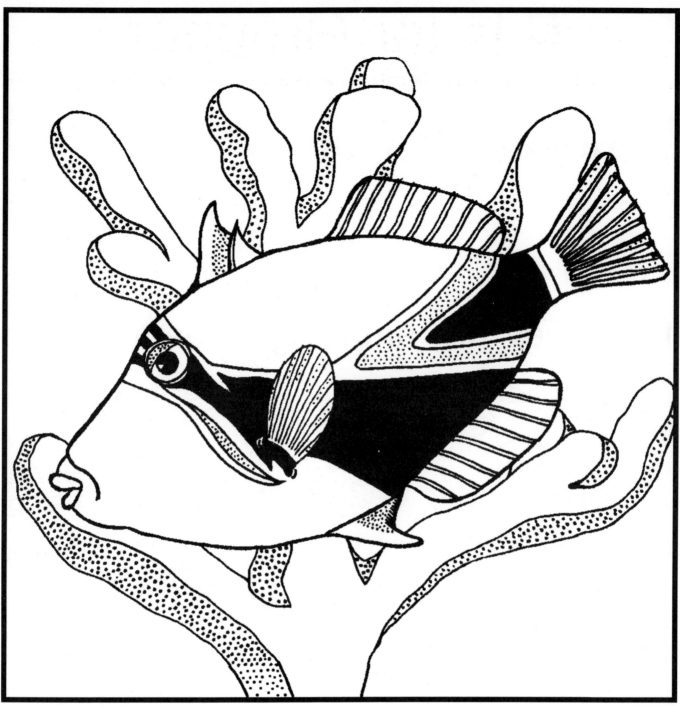

Pig-nosed Trigger Fish   Rhinecanthus rectangulus

H is for
Humuhumu nukunuku apua`a.

H is for
Humuhumu nukunuku apua`a.

The Humu, for short, is Hawaii's state fish. They are amazingly beautiful and look as if someone gently painted them. Their Hawaiian name comes from their snout and the unique piggish grunting noise that they make.

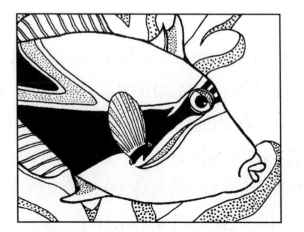

I is for Iheihe.

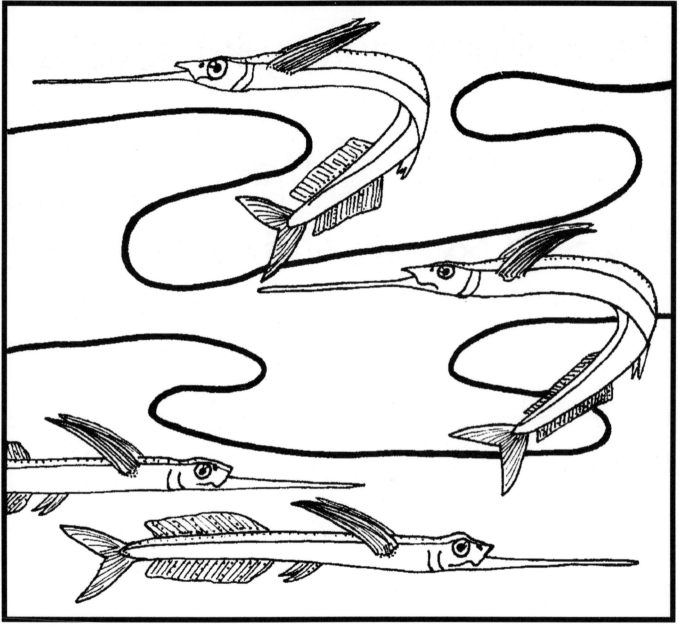

(Green) Half Beak Fish   Ihe ihe   Euleptorhamphus viridis

They are called Halfbeaks because they have short, upper jaws and long, pointy, lower jaws. They are closely related to Needle Fish and Flying Fish. Their bodies are long and slender, like needles. When startled, Iheihe quickly swim along the surface and leap out of the water for short distances.

J is for Jack Fish.

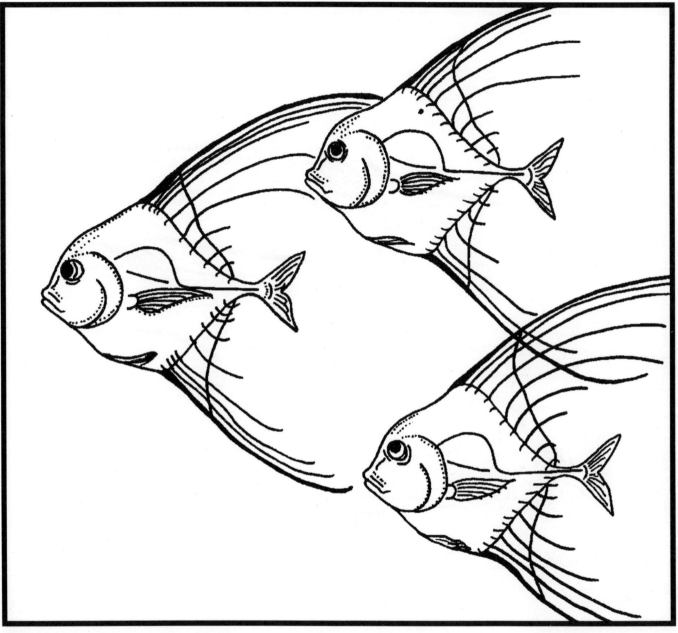

(Thread Fin) Jack Fish   Ulua kihi kihi   Alectis ciliaris

The gorgeous, diamond shaped Ulua kihi kihi are named for their long, thread-like top and bottom fins. As they get older their fins gradually shorten until reaching normal sizes. These rare, silvery fish, which are often called Kagamis, are a sight to behold.

Whitesaddle Goat Fish   Kumu   Parupeneus porphyreus

K is for Kumu.

K is for Kumu.

Kumu are called goatfish because just like billy goats, they have whiskers underneath their chins. They use these whiskers to search for food in the sand and rocks. The colors on their bodies help to camouflage them as they swim about the reef. People in Hawai`i love to eat steamed Kumu.

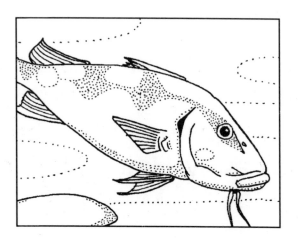

L is for Lion Fish.

Lion Fish

Pterois sphex

Lion Fish are beautiful and colorful, but they are also dangerous. Lion Fish protect themselves with their poisonous dorsal spines. Their bright colors warn other fish to stay away. Hawai`i has a unique species of its own.

 is for Moorish Idol.

Moorish Idol   Kihikihi   Zanclus cornutus

Moorish Idols are called Kihikihi in Hawaii. These peculiarly shaped fish have long thread-like dorsal fins. Kihikihi are seen daintily swimming along the reef. They are often considered Hawaii's most beautiful fish.

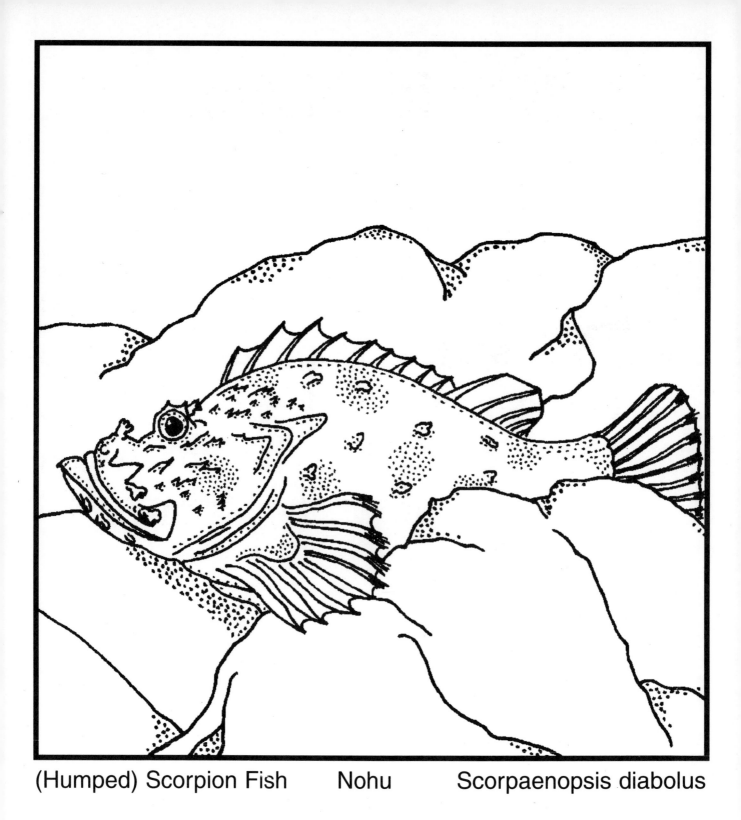

(Humped) Scorpion Fish   Nohu   Scorpaenopsis diabolus

N is for Nohu.

N is for Nohu.

These relatives of Lion Fish also have poisonous spines. Nohu are so ugly that they sometimes look like rocks. They have extra large mouths which they use to gulp down their dinners.

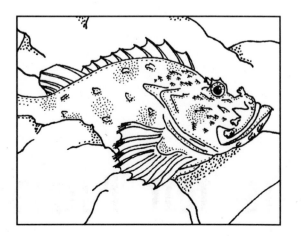

Blue Jack Fish   `Omilu   Caranx melampygus

O is for `Omilu.

O is for `Omilu.

`Omilu, just like Ulua kihi kihi, are Jack Fish. Unlike their relatives, `Omilu have shorter fins which are brilliant blue. They also have bluish-black spots that appear as they get older. `Omilu are great fighters and are one of Hawaii's favorite game fish.

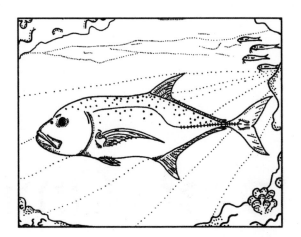

(Red and Violet) Parrot Fish   Uhu   Scarops rubroviolaceus

P is for Parrot Fish.

P is for Parrot Fish.

Their name comes from their beaks and brilliant colors. Uhu actually eat coral! They have special grinders in their throats which crush the coral, producing sand. In fact, many of the beaches in Hawai`i were made by Uhu.

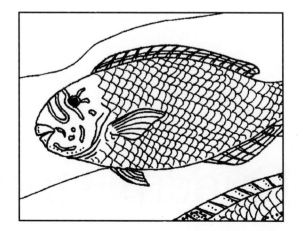

Queen Rudder Fish   Nenue pala   Kyphosus cinerescens

Q is for Queen Rudder Fish.

Q is for Queen Rudder Fish.

Nenue pala is the Hawaiian name for Queen Rudder Fish. They are a rare variety of Nenue. Nenue are normally a drab gray, but Nenue pala are a brilliant golden yellow. These Sea Chubs are not all that chubby! They are actually fairly thin.

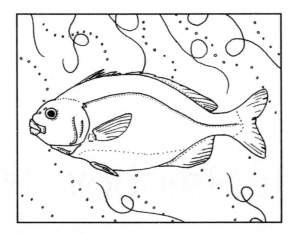

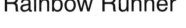 Rainbow Runner   Kamanu   Elagatis bipinnulatus

 is for Rainbow Runner.

R is for Rainbow Runner.

Kamanu look like swimming rainbows with their multicolored, striped bodies. They are often seen swimming with sharks. Kamanu are open ocean fish and are only occasionally seen close to shore.

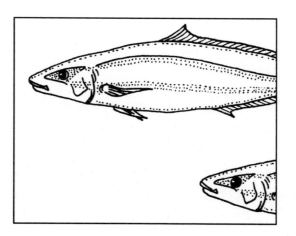

S is for Surgeon Fish.

(Sandwich Island)Surgeon Fish   Manini   Acanthurus sandvicensis

In Hawaiian, these fish are called Manini. They are known for their distinctive color pattern. Manini have six black, vertical stripes on a greenish-gray background. Manini are shallow water reef fish that are only found in Hawai`i.

T is for Ta`ape.

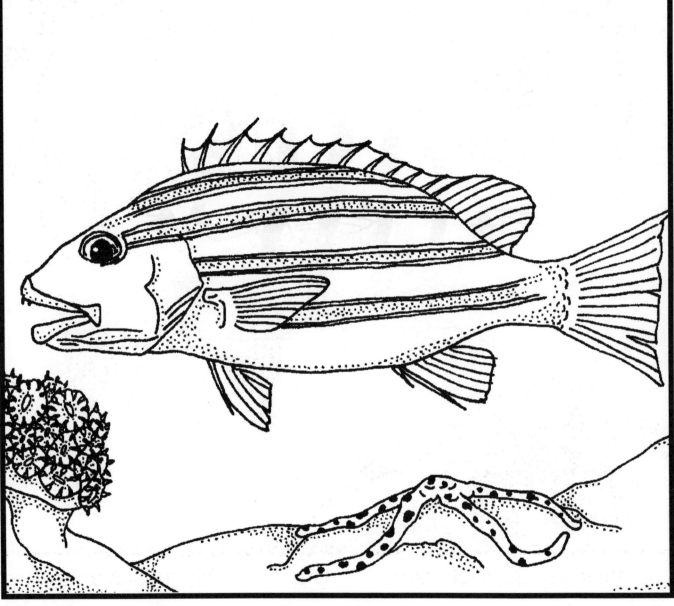

Blue-lined Snapper   Ta`ape (Tahitian)   Lutjanus kasmira

These Snappers have four electric blue, horizontal stripes. They do not have a Hawaiian name because they are not originally from Hawai`i. Ta`ape were introduced from the Marquesas Islands in 1958 and are now found throughout all the Hawaiian Islands.

(Castelnau's) Squirrel Fish   U`u   Myripristis amaenus

U is for U`u.

U is for U`u.

They are blood-red in color. During the day, they spend their time hiding in caves and crevices. At night, U`u come out to search for food. Their large eyes help them to see in the dark.

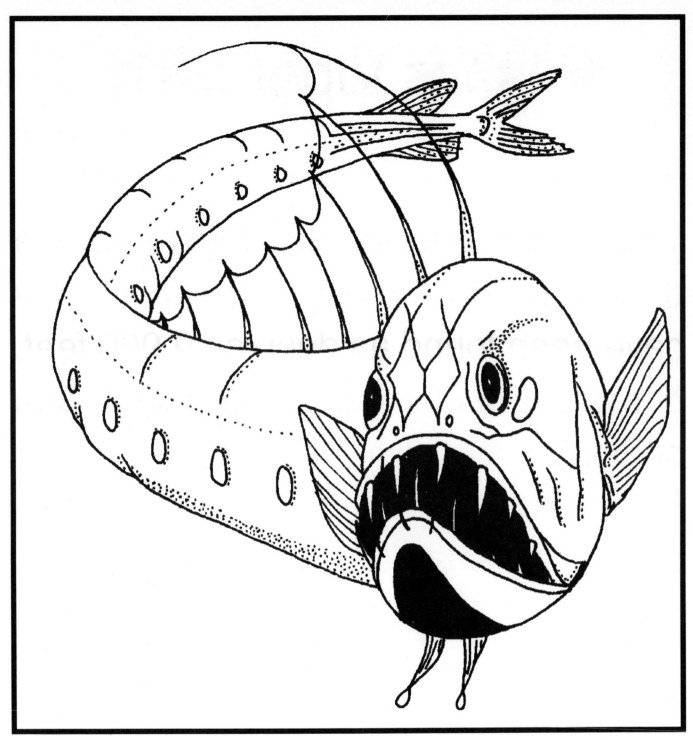

(Sloan's) Viper Fish   Chauliodus sloani

 is for Viper Fish.

V is for Viper Fish.

Viper Fish live at the bottom of the ocean, where it is deep and dark. They have been found as deep as 9,000 feet. Not many people have ever seen them, but they look like little monsters. Viper Fish glow in the dark, and their teeth are terribly sharp.

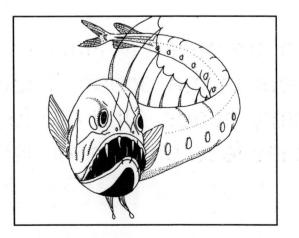

W is for Wahoo.

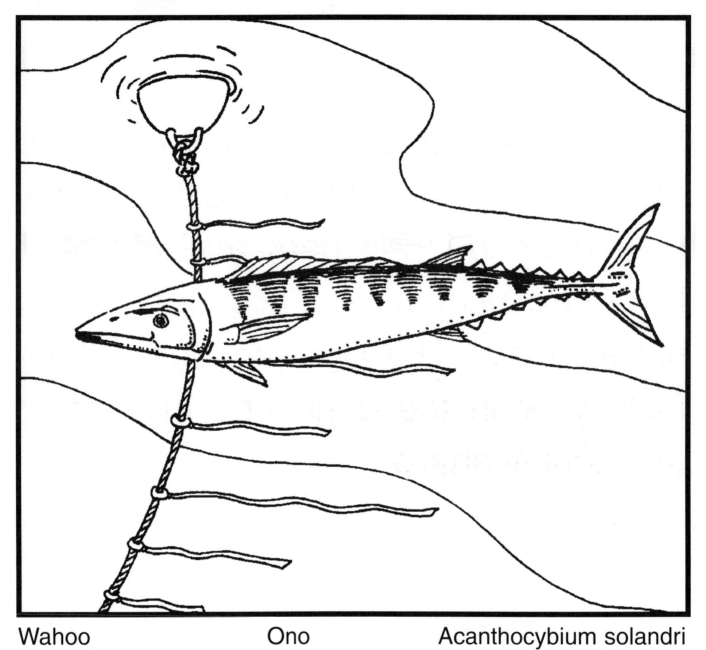

Wahoo   Ono   Acanthocybium solandri

Ono, as Wahoo are called in Hawai`i, are one of the fastest swimmers in the ocean. They have tiger-like stripes and pointy heads. Ono are found in the open ocean where they feed on smaller fish and squid.

X is for Xyrichthys niveilatus.

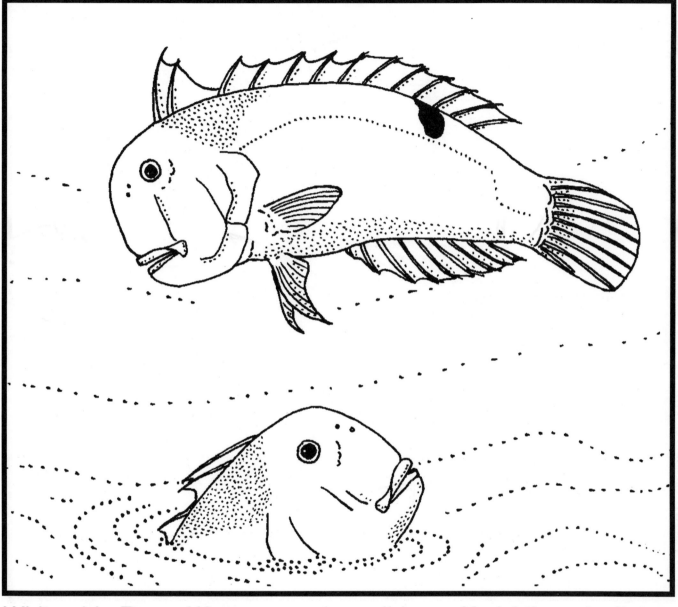

White-side Razor Wrasse   Lae nihi   Xyrichthys niveilatus

What kind of name is this? It is the scientific name of the Lae nihi. Lae nihi have flattened bodies and sharp knifelike foreheads. In fact, Lae nihi means "sharp forehead" in Hawaiian. They are found in areas with calm, sandy bottoms. Lae nihi are usually called by their Japanese name, Nabeta.

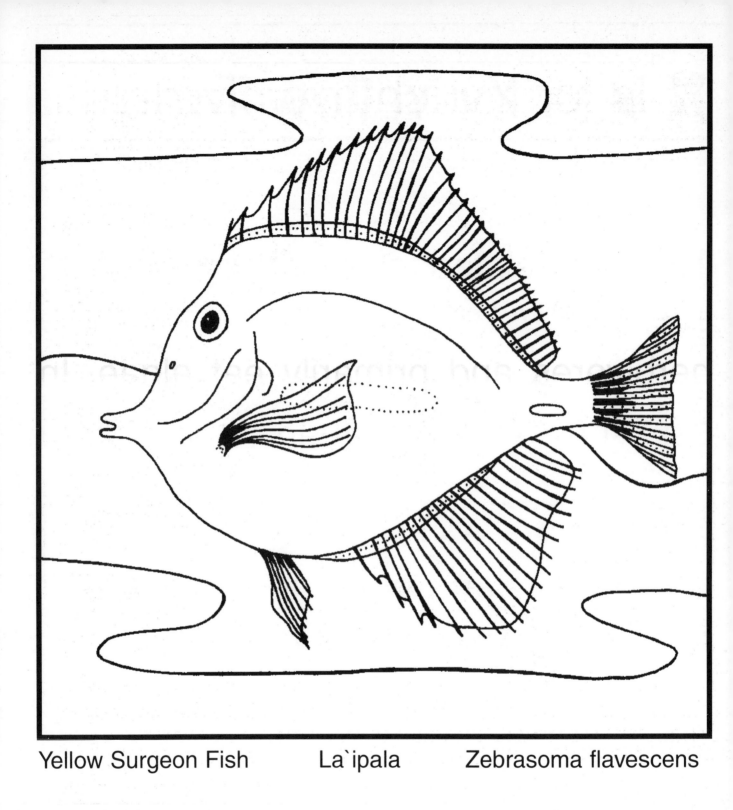

Yellow Surgeon Fish   La`ipala   Zebrasoma flavescens

Y is for Yellow Tang.

Y is for Yellow Tang.

They are related to other Surgeon Fish, such as the popular Manini. They are herbivores and primarily eat algae. In Hawai`i, Yellow Tangs are called La`ipala, which means yellowed ti-leaf. La`ipala are such a bright yellow that they even stand out among other reef fish.

Z is for Zebra Blenny Fish.

Zebra Blenny Fish   Pao`o   Istiblennius zebra

Pao`o are found in tide pools along the shoreline. They are often called Rock Skippers because they have the amazing ability to jump from tide pool to tide pool. Pao`o can also stay out of the water for short periods of time.